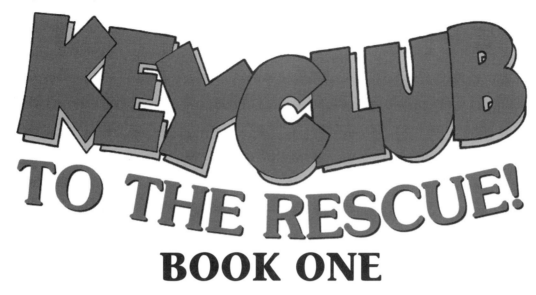

KEYCLUB
TO THE RESCUE!
BOOK ONE

by Ann Bryant

for Rachel Friday, with love

Editor
Louisa Wallace

Cover design by
John Good Holbrook Ltd.

Illustrations by
Paul Selvey, John Good Holbrook Ltd.

Music Setting by
Barnes Music Engraving Ltd.

Published 2001

International
MUSIC
Publications

© **International Music Publications Ltd.**
Griffin House, 161 Hammersmith Road
London W6 8BS
England

Caring for the Environment
This book has been produced with special regard to the environment. We have insisted on the use of acid-free, neutral-sized paper made from pulps which have not been elemental bleached and have sought assurance that the pulp is farmed from sustainable forests.

About this book...

The pieces in **KEYCLUB TO THE RESCUE BOOK ONE** are designed as reinforcement for **KEYCLUB BOOK ONE**, helping your pupils overcome troublesome patches whilst developing and maintaining sight-reading skills.

All the pieces are short, repetitive and almost entirely free of fingerings, which helps train the pupil to look ahead. There are no dynamics, tempo indications or expression marks, making it easier to concentrate on the notes. Each new note appears in the same Keyland area as it does in the tutor book. All the common note patterns for this level are used so the pieces can be mastered easily and the book revisited time and time again as a sight-reading aid.

Pitched at a slightly easier standard than the tutor equivalent, these pieces fall somewhere between sight-reading exercises and ordinary short pieces for practising. There is none of the dryness of typical sight-reading guides here, just all the fun of the Keyclub series with a whole wealth of Keyland characters, familiar and new!

CONTENTS

Climbing Clarence

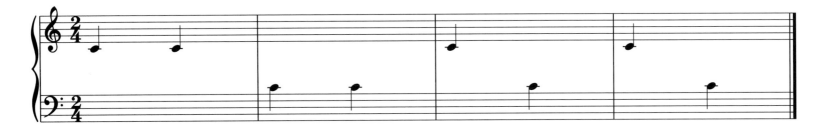

Sliding Sid

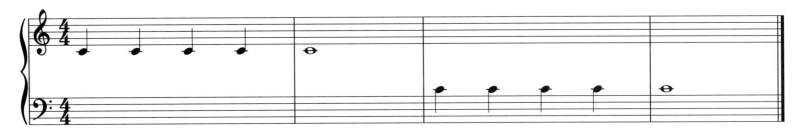

Swinging Susie

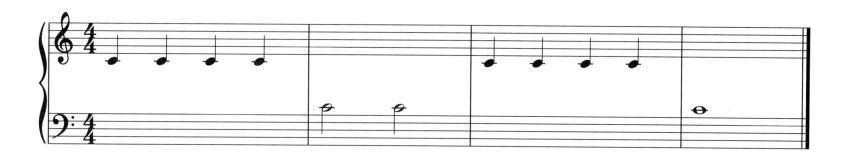

Daring Don

Step up   Step down

The Back-To-Front-Helmet Man

Francesca the Flaming Torch Juggler

Josh the Jet Man

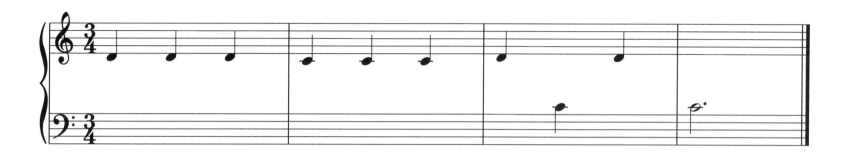

Jumping Jack

Check-Out Charlie

Trevor the Trolley Loader

Pam the Packer

Sam the Stacker

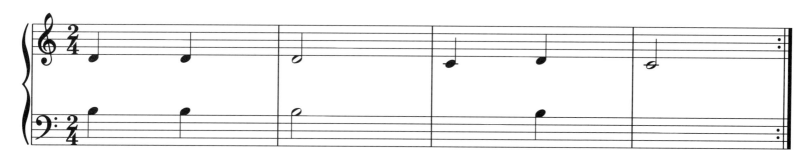

Barney the Baker

Fred the Fishmonger

Bella the Butcher

Marlene the Manager

Skip up

Skip down

Mrs Head the Head Teacher

Dr Bunsen the Chemistry Teacher

Mrs Palette the Art Teacher

Mr Horn the Music Teacher

Sally Sprint the P.E. Teacher

Kevin Kiln the Pottery Teacher

Mrs Microscope the Biology Teacher

Mr Atlas the Geography Teacher

Hayley Hen

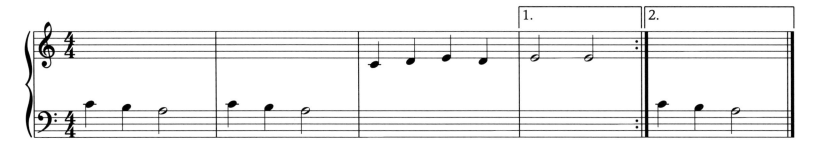

Patelly the Pig

Debra Duck

Horace the Horse

Georgia
Hands together

Tom the Old Tractor

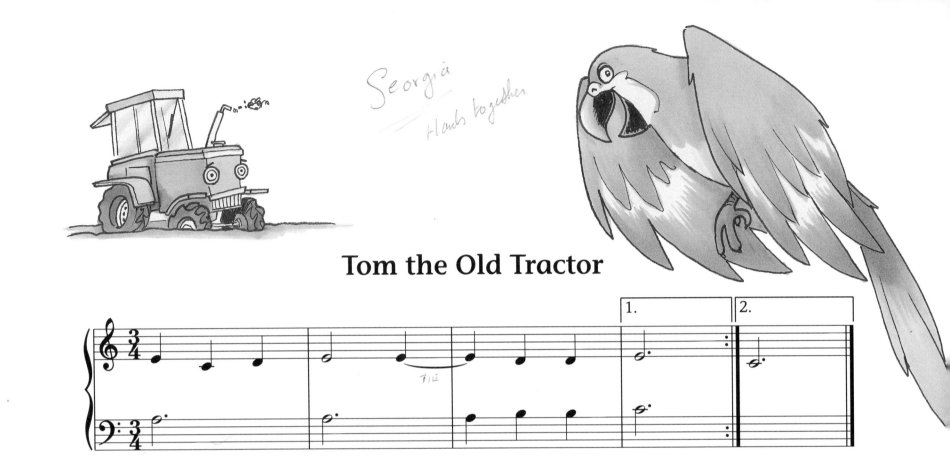

Pauline Parrot

18

Tony Turkey

Khaki the Kid

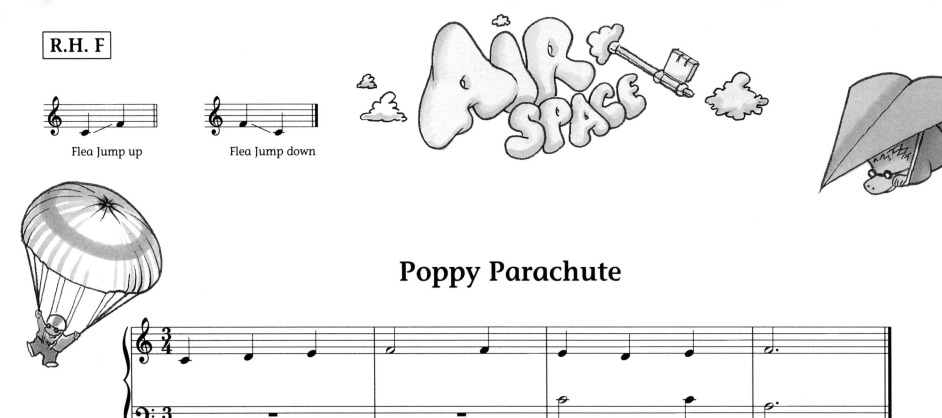

Flea Jump up

Flea Jump down

Poppy Parachute

Howard Hanglider

Raymond Rocket

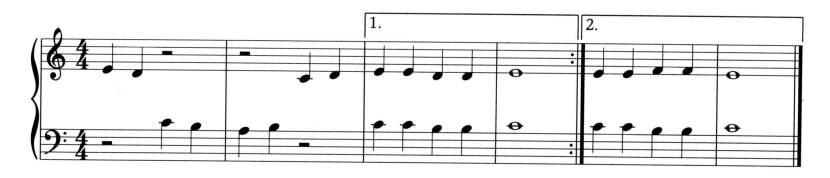

Winston Wings

Snoopy Skyscraper

Hetty Hot Air Balloon

Marilyn Mud Monster

Meredith Mud Monster

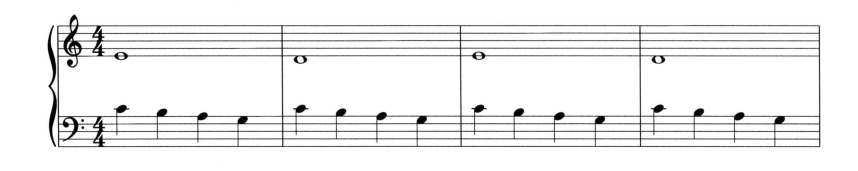

Mini Mud Monster

Hush-a-bye Slush Mud Monster

Frog Jump up   Frog Jump down

Peter Punk Pixie

Ed the Elf

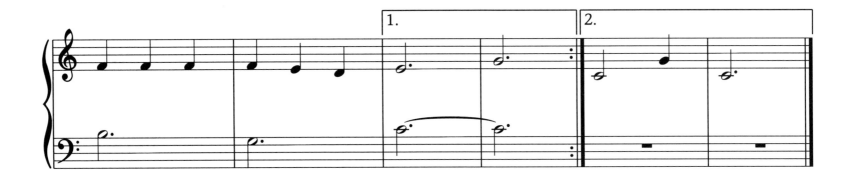

Shaney the Sprite

Norman Gnome

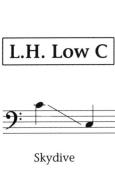

L.H. Low C

Skydive

Beryl Big-Wig

Signor Scraggini

Choose your best R.H. fingerings!

Doris Drone

Prunella Posh

Printed and bound in Great Britain 4/01

by Ann Bryant

Ref: 3582A

Ref: 3583A

Ref: 3584A

Ref: 5469A

Ref: 5470A

Ref: 5471A

Ref: 5847A

EVERY YOUNG PERSON'S FIRST PIANO COURSE

At last a piano course that's up to date, fun to use and packed with pieces to play, things to do and stickers to stick! The KEYCLUB Course takes place in Keyland – a magical fantasy world of characters and places. KEYCLUB however, is more than just a piano course.
It's a real kids' club that every young person can join!

KEYCLUB More Than Just a Piano Course